Saving: How to Save Your Money?

Book 2 of Money: Learning the Basics

Joseph Evaldi

The Books from the Series
Money: Learning the Basics

Going Broke: Learning from Financial Mistakes (Money: Learning the Basics Book 1)

Saving: How to Save Your Money (Money: Learning the Basics Book 2)

Budgeting: How to Budget Your Money (Money: Learning the Basics Book 3)

Retirement: Start Thinking About Your Retirement (Money: Learning the Basics Book 4)

Disclaimer

Otherwise, have fun reading this book. I hope it gives you some ideas that you can use.

Table of Contents

Acknowledgements

I would like to thank my brother Ed Evaldi, who was influential to me with understanding finances. When I was younger, he wanted me to understand the markets and he got me to thinking about money in a different way. I didn't appreciate it then, but that information was valuable even if I didn't do anything with it at that time.

Second, I want to thank a friend of mine who I met in the Creative Writing Class. He introduced me to the book *The Richest Man in Babylon*. Even though, I applied these concepts at the beginning and I grew in wealth, but because of circumstances, I didn't apply them until now.

Lastly, I want to thank all the material that I listened to about saving. You have been helpful with my research in this project. I'm not mentioning everyone here, but the YouTube communities with videos have been helpful. Thank you.

Introduction

How do you save money? In my first book I taught you why we go broke? If you read my book you understand that there are many ways we can go broke and you will understand that you need to understand about saving money or at least not spending more than you make.

If you're picking up this book because you need more tips on how to reinforce your saving skills, then this is a book for you.

I have to tell you wherever you are at life 18 years old in a few years this is a book for you. Bottom line we all need to know saving tips.

If you're downloading this book you're asking the question, how do I save money? You have how many expenses and you don't know where to start. I have to tell you this is a skill we are all improving on.

I first want to tell you my story and enforce to you why saving is important. I didn't take the advice when I was younger. I read a book that said at least 10% needs to be saved for retirement or to be saved in *The Richest Man of Babylon*. It was the beginning and I didn't head that advice. I saved, but not much. I am now 35 years old and I made a lot of mistakes with money.

I had a mental health problem pop up from time to time in my life. In 2006 and 2007, I battled two addictions. And I had given money freely to friends or a spiritual healer. Bottom line, I made mistakes and went broke. I am starting all over with my money, with only some money put away for my retirement.

However, I am making changes in my life and I am sharing them with you. There are some tips that I have learned from others and by self teaching myself.

It is not an expert in this field and you could choose whatever pointers work for you. This is how this book should be used. Maybe you'll find that one thing that can be used the rest of your life.

The truth is we all need to learn how to save and there are tricks of how to do it. You will learn it here. Enough of the talk about saving, let's get into discussing how to save money.

1

Basics about Saving Money

There is one major rule with saving money and that is you want to spend less than you make and have your money work for you.

Many people feel the 401K or Social Security will be good for them, but that is not enough and as I'm learning more, there is additional fees attached to our savings that we don't know about. This is why the second rule is having your money make more money.

However, before I discuss the retirement which will be in another book. I want to discuss what is saving money.

Saving Money is putting money aside for another day and let it accumulate. It is not spending it until you want something or absolutely need it. This is saving money.

Why is saving money important? If we don't discipline ourselves to save money and then find a way to make us more money, then we will be broke. And even if we will just save, we need to think of the future. With money we can get out of bad situations that happen to us.

What if we lose our job, we have money saved up that will help us afford our rent or other expenses. Without this money we will be screwed. I will discuss the importance of the emergency fund next chapter.

Another tip about money is by cutting out expenses. This is one that may backfire, but if you do this right, then it might not hurt you. This will be discussed in another chapter.

Another chapter will be setting up other funds for your money. For example, you could start a gift fund, a fun fund, or another fund. You can plan for the future.

The future is not planned for and it should. We don't think of what needs to be in place and we don't think of what we will need so we live for today. This is a poor way of thinking. I thought like this and I went in debt. This is why I am adopting better saving habits.

It is only a start of what can be financial freedom and that is something that we all can achieve if we are smart about it.

This is some basics about saving money. In the next chapter I will discuss about the emergency fund and the importance of it and what you should do to achieve it.

2

Having an Emergency Savings Fund

What happens if there are problems? Let's just say you get laid off from the job, your car breaks down, or something in your house breaks down. These are cases where you need an emergency fund saved up.

There are benefits in having an emergency fund. The ideal emergency fund would be up to three or six months savings saved up. The savings would consist of each paycheck with that time period.

It may be difficult to save money especially if you are working a job that only pays you $200 for two weeks. And you may wonder how can I survive with this little amount? I have bills to pay and it is tough to save money. How do I get ahead?

I wonder this same question. That is why I am writing now. In the meantime, I save my change and wrapped them up for when I need them. I will discuss this in detail in another chapter. This can go in the bank for your savings.

Also, if you use your card, the left over change could go into the savings account and all you have to do is to not touch the money.

Another thing you can do to build up your emergency fund is take your left over money and then put it into your savings.

Any of these ways are good ways it put money aside and the object is not to touch it. I learned this from experience. I always touched it and from experience there was a time in need that I could have used it. It's better to be prepared than sorry. And this is what the emergency fund will do.

You don't want to have that worry over your head.

In an emergency savings fund you release a little stress. And you may say I don't have the money to do that or I can't afford it. The truth is people who are higher earners have more debt than those who are poor.

Those who are poor might not have the liquid funds, but they are limited in what they could buy and don't take that chance to take out a credit card. So they are frugal with what they spend.

The middle class have liquid funds, but they think they can afford it which will cost them to go broke. They don't think that much about saving or if they do it is in retirements. If they do, they are planning on escaping the middle class.

An emergency fund is needed no matter what status you are. It takes discipline and controlling your impulses. This is why most people go broke. Having discipline is needed with your money. You don't have to be a slave at your job; you can use that job to propel you to where you want to go. And discipline is a key ingredient. And discipline is needed in cutting back on some of the things that you might enjoy. I will discuss that in the next chapter.

3

<u>Saving by Making Cut Backs</u>

We all need to make cut backs on things if we are going to finish ahead. In cut backs I don't mean deprive yourself altogether of everything. Because when you deprive yourself, you will indulge and then go broke. This is not the approach. However, still some things need to get cut back.

<u>Coffee</u>

I love my coffee. I love going to The Coffee House or occasionally going to a Starbucks. And there drinks cost me $3 to $6 depending on if my fiancée gets a drink. However, there is a way we can cut back on what we get.

Maybe there is a way to cut back and not get that large size drink and downsize to a medium hot coffee. This costs maybe $2 and change which the left over change can be saved up for a later date.

Also, another thing that can be done is buying coffee from the store and brewing it yourself or having your significant other make it for you. This can be done for two days or more depending on how much you want to cut back.

However, with me, I like going to coffee shops because I like to write there and coffee and writing go hand and hand. For everyone, it is different. This is just some ideas. I know it might be difficult to cut out on if you are used to it, but consider it a change in routine.

Coffee is not the only thing you can cut out on. Fast food is another thing you can cut back on.

Fast Food

This one is not only a healthy choice, but it could save you money. Fast food might be something we get when we don't feel like making ourselves food. However, it is a costly one.

Maybe you don't want to cut out on fast food altogether, that's ok. You could put yourself on a regiment where you cut out Monday through Thursday or Sunday through Thursday and limit Fast Food to two or three days a week.

This can be away to cut expenses and start saving. It's about 6 to 7 dollars per person for fast food and if you're paying for another person it could get expensive. This is reasons why I am writing right now.

We don't think of these things and we then think

afterwards and ask why are we broke. Eating fast food is why we are broke.

Cut Back on Cable

With Cable TV, it is expensive. You could get satellite TV for the channels you want and save expenses. If you don't watch Cable TV you could get Netflix for $7.99 or Hulu Plus. There are also other networks that can be streamed now to. This is where the world of entertainment is headed anyway.

For example, for months I have had a subscription to Gaiam TV and the WWE Network, but I cancelled the Gaiam TV for lack of money. I remember I once paid $50 for a pay per view for wrestling and now I pay $9.99 for a package of wrestling. It is worth it.

Only thing on Cable WWE Raw and shows on TV Land, and if I invested money in Everybody Loves Raymond and Kings of Queens and WWE Raw was streamed I wouldn't need Cable TV. Plus with YouTube you could find out what happen so I might not need Cable TV altogether.

There are alternate means of entertainment and it can be replaced. This is ways to think about.

If Your Bold, The Internet

The Internet is something that can be cut. I know what you are saying. I can't cut the internet it is something that I need. I can't do without it. Well maybe there is a way that you can't cut it out all together.

There are Coffee Houses such as Starbucks or in my area The Coffee House where there is free internet. And also, they have internet at other places as well. If you have internet on your phone you could look up stuff there. There is a way around and use the internet.

This is if you are bold. I know some might not want to cut it out, but if you are cutting back expenses. This is a way to do it.

Wrapping up the Chapter on Cutbacks

I gave you some suggestions that will help out a lot. These four expenses alone will put money in your pocket. I know at least with the small expenses there is a calculator on an app called the latte factor by David Bach. It was awhile ago since I had it, but you can track your small expenses and it will help. If it's not under the latte factor, look up David Bach and something will pop up.

I know I need to change some habits and in writing this

book it is helping me to understand it better. The bottom line with expenses is cutting back on what you don't need.

Enough of the painful stuff of saving and the stuff we might not want to do, but I'm going to get to in the next chapter, the fun part of saving money. If you don't think saving money is fun, when it accumulates and you start putting your funds together, it gets better. So have fun learning abcut the fun fund in the next chapter.

4

The Fun Fund: The Fun Part of Saving Money

Things get better with the fun fund or the dream fund. Once we save up and put some money aside, we can do the things we dream of.

Money is meant to be spent on the things you truly want. Sometimes we act out of impulse and get the things we don't want or later regret it. With putting money aside on a fun fund you could save up for that wedding, for that house, and for other things that you might want.

How do you start a fun fund? It could be putting aside in a separate fund a small percentage of your paycheck for this fund. It is up to you how much percentage you want to put aside. Eventually, someday you will have the perks of that fund.

Just think of the perks of this fund. It can be travel. It can be a nice date with your significant other. It can be going to a seminar you want to go to or even do a lot more things. Having a fun fund can even mean going to a restaurant you might want to go to.

Christmas Fund

I know this might not have anything to do with the fun fund, but it is important to think of things like this.

I know this is important, because if you don't have any money from your job, you need to plan ahead. I didn't this past year and I am in debt with my former job. That is why I am going to start in the beginning of the year putting money aside. I will speak more on how you can do this in my last chapter.

Having this fund is important. You don't want to be left struggling for last minute gifts because you are without money. It is a horrible feeling around Christmas time. I know this to be true. I felt that feeling this year, but I took out a loan out of my 401K which is a mistake, because you are a slave to your job until you pay it off.

Thinking ahead with these things is important. It is better to be prepared, than not prepared. We need to think ahead with these future expenses.

There are many things we can do with funds. In the next chapter, I will discuss some other tips of saving money. I've discussed the importance of the emergency fund, making cut backs, and having a fun fund and now I will give you some tips that will help you to save in every way I could think of.

5

Some Other Tips on Saving Money

In this chapter, I will discuss some other tips with saving money. You can do these tips if the others don't work out. If you are doing this right now, great maybe this will reinforce it as it is doing with me right now.

Keep it Automated

In keeping it automated, the bank could automatically take out some money from your account and put it there. The object is not to take it out.

Having it automated, you could even put about 10% even more in your 401K or any other retirement account. The person who wrote a book about keeping it automated was David Bach. This is simply putting money aside and let it accumulate without thinking about it.

This is a good approach to saving your money. I am starting to pay myself first and this could help me in the long run. I was thinking life was a sprint before, but success is more like a marathon. For people like us who read or me who is writing this book. Life should be taken like a marathon and treated like it.

I know many of us are not guaranteed tomorrow, but we should not think of ourselves, we should think of who we can help. I know we don't think like this, but it will save a lot of headaches in the long run.

Putting Left Over Money in the Savings Account

Money should be a game we all play. And we can make a game out of not spending every cent we own. We could put what is left over in our bank and put it towards our savings and the night before we get paid.

This is a way to put a plan into action for your emergency fund or whatever fund you are creating. This is putting a plan into action and guaranteeing that you will have money when you need it. I don't know where I heard this before, but it is a good tip.

Saving Your Change

I heard on a YouTube video by Scrapping4aDart before that you could save your change for a year and then using that money for Christmas and then what is left over for savings.

Saving our change is good. It could come in handy

when we need it and the trick here is letting it accumulate.

This could be another plan and trick for saving money. You have a plan and a backup plan. This is how you can benefit in the long run.

Putting Left Over Cash in a Safe

There are ways where at the end of the pay period or week when you do your budget. With whatever is left over you could put in the safe and let it accumulate.

You can do whatever with this fund. The object is to hold on to it as long as possible or whenever you need it. This is the trick in saving money.

I am sure there are other tricks in saving money. In the final chapter I will give a brief summary of all the ideas discussed in this book. I hope they will help you out on your journey. I know they will for me in the future.

Conclusion

There are many tricks in saving money and there are many tips to put your money aside for a rainy day. Rather it is putting your money away in an automated way or saving your change. The trick is not to touch it and let it build up.

There are more tips; I only gave you a few. I'm sure with research you can learn other ways to save money. It is only up to you to do this.

One final tip along you saving travels and that is you can live your life day to day or you can plan for the future and relax a little.

I once heard a statement a long time ago that says, "Chance favors the prepared mind." The same can be said about money. It is something that works us into stress and it is something we strive after, but we truly don't see the damage it does to us.

We could make money in any way. We could be down to 6 hours a week because they are cutting hours at work which happened to me and the next second someone we know will offer us a job to help them out. It is just the job market we are in right now. A friend told me this yesterday as I was writing this as I was talking to him.

What works for our parents doesn't work for us and if you are retired you know you are working more because it is not easy to retire because they didn't plan that Social Security wouldn't work for them.

People aren't loyal to their companies anymore because it's all about getting ahead and learning skills which is what my friend told me yesterday.

Working in a company till the end might not work anymore, but being a business person and doing your dream will work. It is a chance you have to take, but if you don't do it, you will regret it. This has everything to do with saving.

An example of this is what was written in the book by Dr. Spencer Johnson. In the book he tells a story of two mice who are searching for cheese and two people. The mice found their way through the maze and the two people were complaining that their cheese got moved until they had to move around the maze to find their cheese.

Cheese could mean anything. It could mean settling with your situation or it could be moving with the change of life. Cheese could mean money or something else. We have to move with life or we will get stuck.

This story is true with what we think about money, maybe I am like the person who is stuck in the maze and not getting out of their job expecting things to change and that is why I am stuck, but at the same time I am doing something with my writing which is my dream. I am finding an alternative way to the cheese.

This has a lot to do with our thinking of our job, and with discipline it has a lot to do with money. If we do the same thing over and over it won't work after awhile. Someone will move our cheese and other people will get it.

This happened in 1929 and it happened in 2008. People thought their money would last and they didn't plan, they lived for today and I was one of those people. Or maybe they planned, but their broker told them they were ok, but they weren't. Then the crash happened. I wasn't there 1929, but I was there in 2008 as everyone was. I was making mistakes like everyone else and I didn't plan.

Now the market is different and you have to be smart and a super mind to live. You are on a test with everything and also, you can't accomplish everything in a day. We are far busier than before and we need essentials like a computer to live in today's world.

This is why it is very important to plan ahead and start with a plan for your future. Everything is uncertain now and the misconception is that everything will be safe. This is why we have to jump at any opportunity we have in life. We need to ride with the waves of life and we need to plan ahead.

It is simple with a plan that we can prepare and many have been hurt including me with not preparing.

I am writing this book again to reinforce these skills onto myself and if we can pick something up from this book and if you can use some of these tips that this book, then it is a success.

I thank you for reading and please comment on what you think of this book in the comment section. I will greatly appreciate it. If you like it or hate it or even if I need to improve on something. I just want to say again I am not an expert in this field, but these tips could help me and I wanted to share them with you. They might help you.

Preview

Budgeting: How to Budget Your Money (Money: Learning the Basics Book 3)

Introduction

In the first book I discussed about the facts of going broke. The second book I discussed about the importance of saving money. This is the third book in a series of books. In this book I discuss about the importance of budgeting.

Budgeting is debated by people. Some may think it is the next best thing since sliced bread and others may just hate it. Either way budgeting can be an asset if it is used right even if you don't like it.

Like saving money it is a disciplinary tactic that can be used.

What is Budgeting?

Budgeting is where you limit yourself a certain amount a week and stick to the budget. There are benefits to this if you do it. However, there also is a down side to it. Sometimes you might feel limited. All of these points will be discussed in this book.

What will be discussed in this Book?

The first chapter of the book, I will discuss about dividing your check when you are on a budget. The second chapter I will discuss about the importance of living on a budget and sticking to it.

The third chapter I will discuss about resisting the urge of spending your money and rewarding yourself for sticking to the budget.

The fourth chapter I will discuss about the techniques you can use for setting a budget rather it's handwritten or on Excel

In the fifth chapter, I discuss about automating your

budget. So that way you could spend and not worry about it.

Then I discuss about how you know your budget is working and finally wrapping up about the topic on budgeting.

Advice about Reading this Book

This book on budgeting is to give you pointer of what I learned about budgeting. I will tell you what has worked for me and what hasn't. I will also tell you like I told you in the last book that this book is to reinforce these ideas on budgeting into me.

If you follow these tips or are already using them, great. If you're just picking up tips on this book, then this book is for you. However, if you don't like this book and don't want to budget, than that is your decision to make. I am not going to change your decision one way or the other. I just want to add an alternative view. I hope you enjoy and learn all you can read. Enjoy this book.

1

Dividing Your Check and Setting a Budget

It's good to know how much you are spending and where that money is going in order to set a budget. The essentials need to be set.

Every budget is different. From this video by Kendra Atkins, https://www.youtube.com/watch?v=S2ASPqEgV8g, it discusses about the importance of writing down all your expenses, debts, bills, etc. and then work of the list to pay it off. The guy in the video say if you have all your credit card debt or debt, pay the minimum on all of them and then chip away at the smallest debt and it will snowball.

I agree with this. It is a plan for budgeting. Also, by dividing it up you are making sure what is important is getting paid. And the good thing is you could play around with the numbers.

What I do with my budget now is spend for $30 a week for gas now that gas for the car has dropped. I have my phone bill, and my credit card bill. And I am living at home until I could afford to live on my own and then I will adopt other expenses that I will take on.

The key is allocating your money and having some left

over so it can accumulate and setting some money aside so you could spend for the week and enjoy some as well.

Whatever, your expenses are it is good to divide or allocate your check and like I said play around with your numbers. Whatever plan you choose, it's the best plan for you. Rather you give yourself $40 spending money per week or $60. It is up to you, but I will get to that in the next chapter.

Books Written By Joseph Evaldi

Fiction

A Soul Warrior's Journey

The Day at the Bismarck Herald: The Newspaper Reporter War

Christmas Fiction

Finding Christmas: The Story of Joseph

Non-Fiction

Birth Order: How the Roles of Each Sibling are Placed at Birth?

The World of Groups: Sociology and My Experiences in Senior Seminar

The Amazing Effects of Water

The Enlightened Way: How the Zen Path Can Help Treat Depression?

Applying Your Own Interests to Your Boring Job: Can It Be Done?

Poetry

Apparitions of a Warrior

Websites for Joseph Evaldi

http://www.facebook.com/Josephevaldi

https://www.youtube.com/channel/UCSp2TBz566yOGiQfLf
k0Zog

http://www.twitter.com/passageofjoe

http://www.amazon.com/Joseph-
Evaldi/e/B00ONSPVQI/ref=sr_ntt_srch_lnk_1?qid=14179608
24&sr=8-1

About the Author

Joseph Evaldi graduated from Kean University studying Sociology. He ventured in with writing with his book **The Amazing Effects of Water** in 2009.

He then wrote his first novel **A Soul Warrior's Journey** in April 2013. He later finished writing a book of poetry called **Apparitions of a Warrior** in July 2013.

In December 2014, The Amazon Kindle book **Birth Order: How the Roles of Each Sibling are Placed at Birth?** Was the hot new release under Sociology of Marriage & Family for Amazon.

He is currently working on a string of short ebooks which will be released on Amazon Kindle this year.